World Heritage Site

St Kilda

a comparative analysis of the cultural landscape

summary

/ The inhabitants of St Kilda are much happier than the generality of Mankind, being almost the only People in the World who feel the Sweetness of true Liberty. Martin Martin 1698 /

The National Trust
for Scotland

SCOTTISH EXECUTIVE

World Heritage Site
St**Kilda**
a comparative analysis of the cultural landscape
Summary

Based on a comparative analysis of the cultural
landscape of St Kilda prepared at the request of
the World Heritage Committee.

For more information about St Kilda, see
www.kilda.org.uk, or www.hiort.org.uk for the
Scots Gaelic version.

Astron B40137 06/05

ISBN: 0 9546292 8 0

Contents

World Heritage Site
St *Kilda*
a comparative analysis of the cultural landscape
Summary

The special qualities of St Kilda:

1. **Village Bay: Houses, fields and *cleitean***

   * 5000 years of history
   * outstanding preservation
   * survival of a complete system
   * dramatic landscape setting

2. **Dividing the gannet catch**

   * Thriving subsistence based on birds
   * Iconic story of sustainability

3. ***Cleitean* – unique storage structures**

   * Divergent architecture and social system
   * Isolation from the mainstream

4. **Early 20th-century tourists**

   * Superbly documented social history
   * Outside influence and tourism leads to abandonment

> *… it is the combination of landscape and tenure in a difficult terrain which lifts scenery into cultural landscape.* Fowler 2004

Introduction

1

To all who have been there, and many thousands who have not, St Kilda is an amazing place with a remarkable history. A spectacular natural landscape is the canvas upon which people have painted layer upon layer of evidence of their daily survival across the last five millennia.

But this was no ordinary existence. The tiny islands of St Kilda possess two particular qualities which make it appear to us, today, as one of the hardest places on earth where people have settled successfully:

- the islands are extremely wild, remote and isolated, and
- they bear only a handful of natural resources upon which people can survive.

With this combination of adversities, it is surprising to us that people would have wanted – or been able – to live there at all. Yet they did, and the landscape bears testimony to an unusually distinctive, self-reliant hunter/farmer way of life which developed and thrived for at least 5000 years.

The cultural landscape of St Kilda is therefore unique. There are no immediate parallels.

Aerial view of Hirta

St Kilda is currently inscribed on the World Heritage List on account of its outstanding terrestrial and marine natural heritage, and for its landscape value. In July 2004, the World Heritage Committee considered the proposal to extend the World Heritage status of St Kilda to include the cultural landscape that bears testimony to millennia of human endeavour. A decision was deferred at that meeting, and the Committee requested that the comparative analysis in the revised nomination should be enhanced and re-presented.

This document clarifies and amplifies the case put forward in the *Revised Nomination of St Kilda,* looking particularly at the special qualities that give St Kilda its outstanding universal values, and comparing those qualities with other remote communities in the region and further afield. A fuller comparative analysis document, submitted to the World Heritage Centre in December 2004, includes appendices which consider how St Kilda fits into current thinking about World Heritage cultural landscapes. The full submission to UNESCO was accompanied by a document which distilled the cultural heritage extracts from the full Revised Nomination; this gives further detail of the background to the islands' history and management. More information about all aspects of St Kilda can be found on the website www.kilda.org.uk (www.hiort.org.uk for the Gaelic version).

a. Country
United Kingdom

b. State, Province or Region
Western Isles
Scotland

c. Name of Property
St Kilda (Hirta)

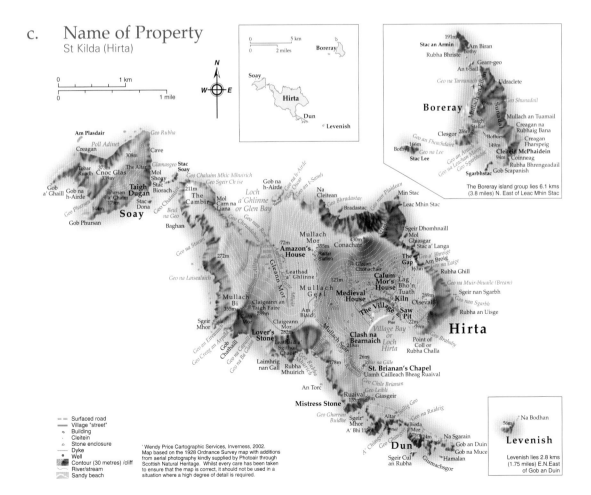

Boreray

Soay

Hirta

Dun

Levenish

N
W E

0   1 km
0   1 mile

0   5 km
0   2 miles

191m
Stac an Armin   Am Biran
Rubha Bhriste   Bothy
                    Gearr-geo
                An t-Sail
Geo na Tarnanach Eilean   Udraclete
                        370m   Geo Shunadail
Boreray
                        Mullach an Tuamail
                Clesgor   230m   Creagan na
            Taigh   Rubhaig Bana
            Stallar Bothies   Creagan
Bothy 166m   149m   Fharspeig
    Geo na Lee   Cleitein McPhaidein
                            94m   Coinneag
Stac Lee   Geo an Aird
            Geo na Leacan Maire
                Geo Sgarbhstac   Rubha Bhrengeadail
                    Sgarbhstac Gob Scapanish

The Boreray island group lies 6.1 kms
(3.8 miles) N. East of Leac Mhin Stac

Am Plasdair   Geo Rubha
Poll Adinet
Creagan   Cave
        308m
Tobar 373m The Altar Glamasgeo **Stac**
Ruadh Cnoc Glas 339m   **Soay**
Gob   Mol   Geo Chaluim Mhic Mhuirich
a' Ghaill Gob na   Shoay   Geo Sgeir Ch ise   Gob na
    h-Airde   Stac 211m   h-Airde
        Phursan a' Chatin Biorach The   Na
Geo Phursan 179m   Stac Mol Cambir Loch   Cleitean
    144m   Dona Carn na   a' Ghlinne
Gob Phursan **Soay** Liana Beul or Glen Bay   Bradastac
                    na Geo   Geo Bhradastac
            Baghaid   Leac Mhin Stac

Geo na Stacan   Sgeir Dhomhnaill
                    Mullach   Mol
            272m   Mor   430m   Ghiasgar
                72m 355m Conachair Stac a' Langa
            Amazon's   Geo a' Bhrosge Am Brosge
Geo na Laisealaich **House** Radar   163m Geo na Eaige
                    Station   Rubha Ghill
            Leathad 121m   Glacan
            a' Ghlinne   Chonachair   Geo na Muir-bhuaile (Bream)
        Mullach   **Calum**
        Geal   **Mor's** Lag   289m Sgeir nan Sgarbh
Mullach Claigeann an **Medieval** **House** Bho'n Geo nan Sgarbh
Bi   Taigh Faire **House** Tuath Oisevall Rubha an Uisge
356m 289m   **Kiln**
    Cam   Am   **The Village** **Saw**
Sgeir Mor Blaid   Pier **Pit** 22m
Mhor   Claigeann   Village Bay   **Hirta**
            Mor 282m or   Point of
    Lover's Leathad Mullach Sgar Loch Coll or
    Stone a' Sgithoil **Clash na** Hirta Rubha Challa
Geo an Eireannich Chaoil **Bearnaich** 218m
Gob Geo na Cailidh   26m
Chabaill   178m Tobar na Gille
Geo Creag an Airbhi   Rubha **St. Brianan's Chapel**
    Laimhrig Mhuirich   Uamh Cailleach Bheag Ruaival
    nan Gall   Geo Chile Brianan
        An Torc   Geo Leibli
                Ruaival 135m Giasgeir
Mistress Stone
        Geo Gharran Sgeir Altar Geo na Ruideig
        Buidhe Mhor   Na Bodhan
            A' Bhi 119m Bioda
                        Mor 124m Na Sgarain 50m
        A' Chlagh Chasda Tunnel   Gob an Duin **Levenish**
                    Dun Geo Ghlusgar Gob na Muce
            Sgeir Cul   Hamalan   Levenish lies 2.8 kms
            an Rubha Giumachsgor   (1.75 miles) E.N.East
                                    of Gob an Duin

Min Stac

= = Surfaced road
— Village "street"
▫ Building
◦ Cleitein
◦ Stone enclosure
▦ Dyke
◦ Well
Contour (30 metres) /cliff
River/stream
Sandy beach

' Wendy Price Cartographic Services, Inverness, 2002.
Map based on the 1928 Ordnance Survey map with additions
from aerial photography kindly supplied by Photoair through
Scottish Natural Heritage. Whilst every care has been taken
to ensure that the map is correct, it should not be used in a
situation where a high degree of detail is required.

1

1. The cleit at 'the end of the world'

2. The Amazon's House: a roofed structure, thought to be prehistoric

3. St Kildan children, evacuated before adulthood

4. The Mistress Stone: where suitors would display their climbing skills

> **Recommendation: re-assessing cultural and natural sites already on the World Heritage List, to ensure that cultural landscape potential is recognized through re-nomination if appropriate**
> WHC 2003

St Kilda – a cultural landscape of World Heritage value

2

2.1 Existing ICOMOS recommendations

In June 2004, following receipt of the *Revised Nomination of St Kilda* and an evaluation visit in 2003, ICOMOS **recommended inscription** of the islands on the following cultural criteria:

> *'Criterion iii:* **St Kilda bears exceptional testimony to over two millennia of human occupation in extreme conditions.**
>
> *Criterion v:* **The cultural landscape of St Kilda is an outstanding example of land use resulting from a type of subsistence economy based on the products of birds, cultivating land and keeping sheep. The cultural landscape reflects age-old traditions and land uses, which have become vulnerable to change particularly after the departure of the islanders.'**

This reinforced an earlier ICOMOS recommendation in 1986, in response to the initial nomination document, where they concluded that 'the St Kilda archipelago corresponds perfectly to the definition of a cultural and natural property…'.

World Heritage Site

StKilda
a comparative analysis of the cultural landscape
Summary

Village Bay, Hirta: the village, with its street, houses, enclosures, *cleitean* and fields, is the best preserved system of its type. But the village only marks the end of a long history of human occupation, evidence of which survives extensively throughout the landscape.

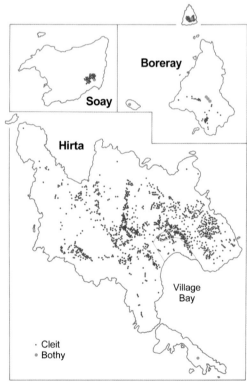

Boreray

Soay

Hirta

Village Bay

· Cleit
• Bothy

The dense distribution of *cleitean* and bothies on all the islands and large sea stacks of the archipelago reveals how the St Kildans utilised every part of the landscape – part of the remarkable legacy of built structures

The 1986 ICOMOS report stated: 'The tiny St Kilda archipelago in the Hebrides Island is not only one of the biggest sanctuaries of wildlife and marine life in the North Atlantic, but also bears testimony to a coherent ecosystem which has remained virtually unchanged over 2,000 years of human occupation. From the Bronze Age to the evacuation of the archipelago's last inhabitants in 1930, the islands of Soay, Hirta, and Boreray, and the islets bordering their coasts have undergone several periods of human occupation. At several sites there is evidence of a Christian influence prior to the Viking invasion, as illustrated by numerous artefacts from the 10th century. Difficult to date, the conserved structures – cairns, circular stone formations, groups of monastic cells and even post-medieval villages – illustrate a remarkable persistence of forms of primitive architecture in a country whose traditional modes of construction have survived to the contemporary period.'

The combined works of nature and man.

World Heritage Convention, Article 1.

2.2   St Kilda's outstanding universal value

To be recognised as a cultural landscape worthy of World Heritage Site status, a place must demonstrate 'outstanding universal value'. For St Kilda this is undoubtedly the case:

The '**universal value**' of St Kilda is as an exceptionally well-preserved and documented example of how, even in the most **extreme conditions** of storm-swept remoteness and very few obvious natural resources, people have been able to live in **harmony with nature** for millennia. The St Kildans led a distinctive social and economic way of life, in response to the peculiar physical and geographic setting of the islands.

However, increasing **external influences** from the 19th century onwards brought aspirations and expectations that eventually made the way of life **no longer sustainable** – leading to the evacuation of the islands in 1930.

St Kilda is of '**outstanding value**' in this context because of:

- the **time-depth**, **preservation** and **completeness** of the physical remains of a whole human system that reflects a distinctive geo-cultural census;

- the remarkable **documentary evidence** of society and traditions that puts flesh on the bones of the archaeological ruins; and

- the **dramatic landscape** to which this cultural wealth integrally contributes, and which has helped give St Kilda its iconic status.

Review of cultural significance: the landscape setting

The dramatic landscape setting, the subject of hundreds of published photographs, is one of the key assets of the cultural landscape of St Kilda. On the largest island, Hirta, the sheer scale of the hills within which the settlements seem to fit perfectly is remarkable. On Boreray, the steepness of the slopes on which prehistoric settlement and later historic summer bothies are set is awe-inspiring. While Stac an Armin, with its *cleitean* and bothy surrounded by the raucous calling of tens of thousands of gannets, is breathtaking. And these are just some of the landscapes that make up the archipelago that is St Kilda.

No relict prehistoric and historic landscape can rival St Kilda in this respect, and the cultural landscape unquestionably contributes to the aesthetic appeal of the landscape, which is already recognised in St Kilda's World Heritage inscription under natural criterion iii. *Revised Nomination of St Kilda 2003*

2.3   Evaluation Checklist

The following checklist (Phillips 1995, 390) of items for evaluation of cultural landscapes for World Heritage status is useful for highlighting the match with St Kilda:

Landscapes as a resource

The landscape should be a resource of world importance in terms of **rarity** and **representativeness**

Scenic quality

The landscape should be of the **highest scenic quality**, with pleasing or **dramatic patterns** and combinations of landscape features, and important **aesthetic** or **intangible qualities**

Unspoilt character

The landscape within the area should be **unspoilt** by large scale, visually intrusive or polluting industrial or urban development or infrastructure

Sense of place

The landscape should have a distinctive and common character, including **topographic and visual unity**

Harmony with Nature

The landscape should demonstrate an outstanding example of a **harmonious interaction between people and Nature**, based upon **sustainable land-use practices**, thereby maintaining a diversity of species and ecosystems

Cultural resources

The landscape should contain **buildings and other structures of great historical and architectural interest**; the **integrity** of these features should be apparent

Consensus

There should be a consensus among professional and public opinion as to the world importance of the area; reflected, for example, through **associations with writings and paintings** about the landscapes which are of international renown.

2.4 St Kilda timeline

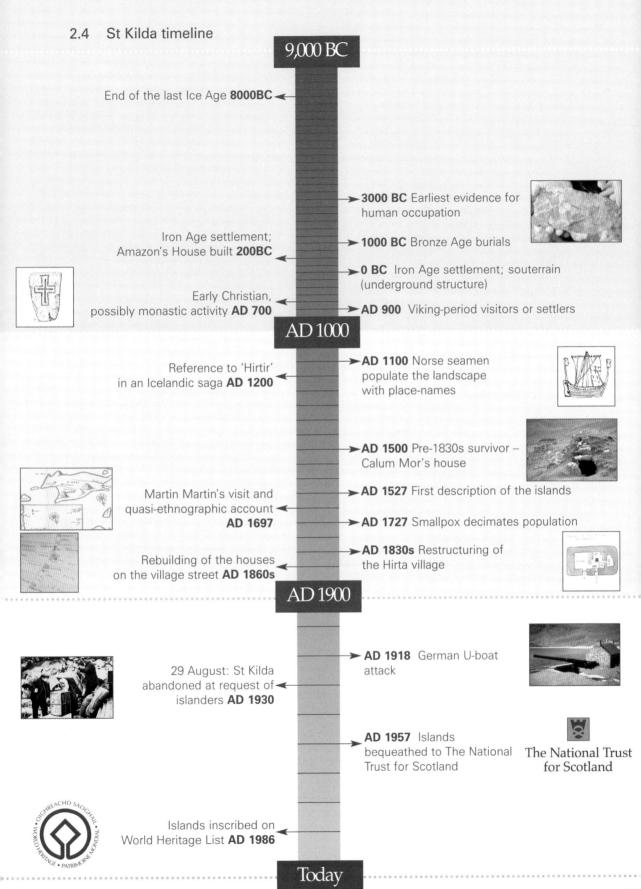

9,000 BC

End of the last Ice Age **8000BC**

3000 BC Earliest evidence for human occupation

Iron Age settlement; Amazon's House built **200BC**

1000 BC Bronze Age burials

0 BC Iron Age settlement; souterrain (underground structure)

Early Christian, possibly monastic activity **AD 700**

AD 900 Viking-period visitors or settlers

AD 1000

Reference to 'Hirtir' in an Icelandic saga **AD 1200**

AD 1100 Norse seamen populate the landscape with place-names

AD 1500 Pre-1830s survivor – Calum Mor's house

Martin Martin's visit and quasi-ethnographic account **AD 1697**

AD 1527 First description of the islands

AD 1727 Smallpox decimates population

AD 1830s Restructuring of the Hirta village

Rebuilding of the houses on the village street **AD 1860s**

AD 1900

AD 1918 German U-boat attack

29 August: St Kilda abandoned at request of islanders **AD 1930**

AD 1957 Islands bequeathed to The National Trust for Scotland

The National Trust for Scotland

Islands inscribed on World Heritage List **AD 1986**

Today

1. The distinctive 'exclosures' at An Lag

2. Roofed bothy on the St Kildan island of Boreray

3. Sharbau's map of 1860, when the village was substantially rebuilt

4. Fowling on Stac an Armin, 1886

©Colin Baxter

> *A cultural landscape is a place where people and Nature have interacted, not just impacted, and the results of that interaction give the landscape in view its particular character.* Fowler 2004

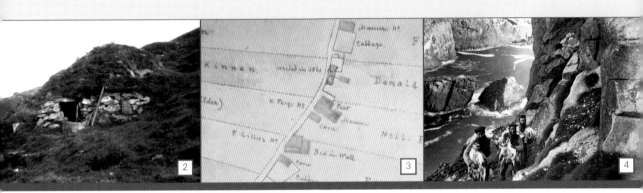

The essentials of a comparative analysis

3

3.1 General characteristics of World Heritage cultural landscapes

Guidance from the World Heritage Centre (WHC 2001, Para. 2.3) makes clear that a comparative analysis should relate the property to comparable places, and indicate:

1. Why it is *more worthy* for inscription on the World Heritage List or, for those already inscribed;
2. What features *distinguish* this property from existing World Heritage Sites;
3. Whether it is intrinsically *better*, or possessed of more features;
4. If it is *better preserved* or a more complete survival; or
5. If it has been *less prejudiced* by later developments.

All of these aspects will be considered in the following analysis.

St Kilda does not fit into well-defined categories of cultural landscape like formal gardens and pleasure grounds, or landscapes associated with wine making or growing rice. However, a recent review of World Heritage cultural landscapes (Fowler 2003, 51), published by the World Heritage Centre, has been helpful in identifying a number of generic attributes (*in bold text*) which are particularly relevant to St Kilda:

'World Heritage cultural landscapes have now begun to define themselves collectively. They are characterised:

One of the hundreds of *cleitean* on Hirta, a lone sentinel over Village Bay

- **Geographically/topographically/ functionally by:**

  mountains, water, farming and inhabited settlements including towns;

- **Intellectually by:**

  historical and/or ***cultural significance, continuity*** and ***tradition, religiosity and aesthetics.'***

The characteristics of St Kilda clearly match extremely well with other cultural landscapes that have already been identified as being worthy of inscription to the World Heritage List, and the level of preservation, documentation and understanding of the way people lived serve to raise St Kilda above most other places in the world.

The following comparative analysis begins with those places nearest to St Kilda in terms of proximity and cultural background. The analysis then looks at places further afield, on the western seaboard of Ireland, and on the north-west fringes of Europe – Norway, the Faeroe Islands, and beyond.

The analysis goes even further afield to look internationally at very remote places with minimal natural resources but which have nevertheless sustained human settlement.

3.2 Principal characteristics of the St Kilda cultural landscape

Before comparing and contrasting St Kilda with other places, it is useful to set out the criteria which will be used for comparative purposes. The characteristics which give St Kilda its outstanding universal value and, in combination, make it unique can be summarised as:

- The time-depth locked within the landscape, representing the occupation of the tiny archipelago over at least five millennia;

- The quality, intensity and completeness of the surviving archaeological and landscape evidence – at system rather than just site level – of this very long occupation and human use of the resources available to them;

- Humanity's survival in very extreme conditions such as the small number of food sources, the inaccessibility of the islands, the harshness of climate and the lack of timber resources;

- The reliance for survival principally on the exploitation of birds, contrasting with the comparative lack of use of marine resources;

- The careful use of natural resources, exemplified by the survival of the Soay sheep which have themselves become a 'living artefact' and an internationally important gene pool;

- The exceptionally good physical evidence for St Kilda's assimilation to a more standard pattern of settlement and contact in the 19th century;

- Outstanding levels of documentation from the 17th century onwards both of the 'indigenous' life style and of the assimilation into the mainstream, and eventual abandonment;

- The distinctive social systems and architectural styles consequent upon this isolation;

- St Kilda's isolation and consequent reliance on a subsistence economy with few trading links up until the 19th century;

- The dramatic landscape setting, to which the cultural landscape features are integral;

- The story of abandonment, precipitated by tourism and other external influences, resulting in St Kilda's iconic status to people from around the world.

1. A paved lane between village houses, preserved to wall-head height

2. The famous St Kilda Parliament in the 1880s – the distinctive form of social organisation

3. Wreck in Village Bay, demonstating why fishing was thought bad luck by the St Kildans

4. Fowling for puffin, using distinctive rods with multiple nooses

> *... if this is not the Eutopia so long thought, where will it be found?* MacCulloch 1819

The Scottish Highlands and Islands context

4

St Kilda is one of many archipelagos in the Highlands of Scotland, but while there are various similarities between these relatively remote outposts of human habitation, the combination of special qualities found on St Kilda make it unique.

The first impression of the island of Hirta is one of an amazing density of stone buildings – houses, blackhouses, *cleitean*, dykes, planticrubs and enclosures. Nowhere else in the Highlands of Scotland is there such an overwhelming presence of constructions from an age past.

Within the most recent settlement area on Hirta, the linear village is characterised by more than 20 blackhouses dating to the 1830s, alternating with 16 houses from the 1860s. The building of these homes in two distinct, short phases and without the large-scale destruction of the earlier constructions is unique to St Kilda. None of these buildings has been enlarged in plan, and no additional structures have been added to the

street since the 1860s. This, too, is unparalleled in Highland Scotland.

Across Hirta, Soay, Boreray and Stac an Armin are many hundreds of *cleitean* – the uniquely constructed stone storage structures which formed a key feature that ensured a food-supply chain for those living on St Kilda for millennia. These structures are only found on St Kilda. Nowhere else are there so many stone storehouses associated with so few homes. Nowhere else do same-function structures exhibit such a variety of shapes, sizes and layouts within such a small geographical area. Nowhere else have stone storehouses amongst regularly-used hunting/gathering grounds proved necessary.

Cleitean, fields and enclosures: the level of survival of the infrastructure of the 19th-century village and its predecessors is exceptional. Archaeological excavations have shown that features going back more than 2000 years are preserved below the hand-cultivated soil – much of which was probably imported from outside the 'head dyke' settlement boundary.

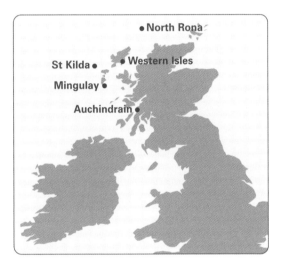

On the north side of Hirta, in Gleann Mor, is a landscape associated with the management of sheep and cattle, overlying a prehistoric landscape of settlement and agricultural use. The form of the features associated with the post-medieval and medieval stock control is unmatched in the Highlands of Scotland. Grazing management elsewhere is characterised by simple shielings (summer grazing areas) in compact groups. In Gleann Mor, however, the 16 complexes of stone 'enclosures', cellular structures and larger underlying prehistoric constructs scattered across the landscape have no parallels.

Medieval or later rural settlement survives notoriously poorly in the Highlands of Scotland, not least because most structures were built of turf and wood. This was not the case on St Kilda, where stone was the main building material. One structure of this period has survived in its entirety on Hirta – Calum Mor's House – which is therefore of outstanding significance. It is known that well-preserved remains of similar structures survive elsewhere on the island, buried beneath the turf. It is much more usual for the older evidence to have been swept away by demolition and subsequent reconstruction on exactly the same place, or for agricultural activity to have destroyed all traces of what went before.

On Boreray, Soay, Dun and Hirta there is a complexity of prehistoric sites and areas that defy the later notion of a population cut off from the world at large. The survival of such a time-depth is not unusual in the Highlands of Scotland. What is unusual is that it survives as an integral part of a comparatively small area of land which has been so intensively used over the millennia.

The late medieval and post-medieval cultural identity of St Kilda is characterised by an amazing wealth of documentary records. For such a tiny community, this is unique in the archives of Highland Scottish material. Authors describe the egalitarian nature of the society – not paralleled elsewhere in the Highlands and islands – as well as the specific traditions associated with the way of life on the archipelago, particularly relating to the taking of birds from the incredible cliffs and sea stacks.

St Kilda
a comparative analysis of the cultural landscape
Summary

Harris (Western Isles) architecture in 1831: the same juxtaposition of old and new began in the early 19th century on Hirta, but in 1834 the old houses were almost all dismantled to make way for the 'modern' arrangement we have inherited

The importance of the seabird harvest to the people of St Kilda was greater than those of any other island in the Scottish Highlands. This characteristic underpins the uniqueness of the cultural landscape of St Kilda, which spans land, cliffs, and sea.

In a material sense, we wish to compare St Kilda to its neighbours in terms of the level of survival, time-depth and readability of the tangible features of the landscape. In terms of the way of life, we need to compare and contrast the agricultural system that produced the cultural landscape, and also the social organisation that governed the islanders' daily existence. We also need to look at how that existence was affected by the remoteness and relative lack of contact with the outside world.

4.1 The Outer Hebrides context – Scotland's Western Isles

The Outer Hebrides are covered with archaeological sites of all periods, many surviving extremely well although often buried under peat or sand. But as a cultural landscape the islands as a whole do not exhibit a great coherency of survival or preservation through time, unlike the St Kilda archipelago which boasts an incredible density of evidence from all periods, often with exceptional levels of survival – both above and below ground.

In addition, the Outer Hebrides do not have a history of dependence on a particular food-supply chain. Everywhere in the Outer Hebrides is reliant on fishing and small-scale farming, but only on St Kilda was there such a dependence on seabirds – their eggs, meat, oil and feathers.

While the medieval and later tenurial system of the St Kilda archipelago was the same as that on the Outer Hebrides, socially there were significant differences. These were manifest in the 'St Kilda Parliament', where the work of the day would be decided by the menfolk, and also in terms of the equitable division of the fruits of the day's communal labours. Such differences were arguably necessary or even vital to the sustainability and survival of this relatively large community living off the bounty offered by the archipelago: the secret of their success in the face of adversity.

Therefore, the magnificent survival and preservation of archaeological and historic structures; the importance of the dependence on the seabirds for food and rent; and the development of a specific social structure all mean that **St Kilda stands apart from other places in the Outer Hebrides**.

Mingulay village in 1909 and Hirta village in 1831: the two villages may once have looked similar, but Mingulay was never 'modernised'

4.2 Mingulay – 'The near St Kilda'

The island of Mingulay, towards the southern tip of the Western Isles, is sometimes referred to as 'the near St Kilda', and in a few ways this comparison is justified. Like St Kilda, Mingulay was evacuated in the first part of the 20th century (1911) when the few remaining islanders were resettled. The comparison with St Kilda is also in part due to the relative remoteness of Mingulay – not in terms of distance from other places, but because of the unreliability of the landing place and the dangerous seas and currents. Even today, like St Kilda, no matter what transport is being used, travellers will only be sure of getting there when their feet touch dry land.

Mingulay village – entombed in sand: The village on Mingulay survives extremely well, in part because many of the huddle of blackhouse shells have been inundated with sand – sometimes to wall-head height. However, it bears no comparison with the village on Hirta which is a complete survival of an 1830s and then 1860s planned settlement with its directly associated fields and storehouses, enclosures and planticrubs.

Ancient beginnings: As with many islands in the Scottish Highlands, recent archaeological survey has revealed a number of significant remains of prehistoric and later date. But the remains on Mingulay appear only to constitute fragments of the former land-use system, and do not have the clarity and readability of those spread across Hirta.

Fishing, fowling and farming: Like St Kilda, fowling was an important activity in the lives and economy of the Mingulay islanders, and the cliffs continue to be home to large populations of seabirds. However, fishing formed a much larger part of the Mingulay economy, as, although still dangerous, the waters around Mingulay are less treacherous than those further out into the Atlantic Ocean. St Kilda is acknowledged as *the* archipelago of seabird hunting.

Corbelled stone structures on North Rona and Hirta:
with an almost complete absence of wood for building,
stone-based construction techniques were similar on
both islands

In comparing the special qualities of Mingulay with St Kilda, we find that **St Kilda excels because**:

- historic and prehistoric structures across the cultural landscape on St Kilda are possessed of more features, and they survive better and are far more complete than those on Mingulay; and

- the tradition of seabird hunting, with its associated structures, folklore and oral traditions, was far more important and more developed on St Kilda than that on Mingulay.

4.3 North Rona – 'The distant isle'

Although much smaller in scale (only 120ha in extent and 107m at the highest point), with much less spectacular topography, the island of North Rona bears some similarities to St Kilda. Just as remote, and with a certain amount of fowling undertaken, the small community on North Rona lived in a tiny cluster of three houses of pre-19th-century origin – on a site with Early Christian remains. Largely abandoned by the late 18th

century, the island has none of the density of structures, extensive evidence for storage, or complexity of time-depth that makes St Kilda so important.

4.4 Auchindrain township

The Highland township of Auchindrain is probably the most intact surviving example of an 18th to 19th-century small nucleated village in Scotland. It has a good resource of documentary and oral accounts of daily life, and has been an open-air museum since 1975. The village is unusual, like the settlement on Hirta, in that it was bypassed by the Highland Clearances, and the buildings remained almost unchanged in outward layout thereafter.

However, Auchindrain completely lacks the isolation of St Kilda and the pattern of buildings is unstructured, in contrast with the cohesion of the 19th-century village on Hirta, although both places share a remarkable degree of intactness. But Auchindrain's associated hinterland of fields and other resources is nowhere near so well

Visitors at Auchindrain Township

preserved as that spread over St Kilda, and hunting formed an almost insignificant part in Auchindrain's very different agricultural economy.

4.5 Hebridean and Highland Scottish comparisons

St Kilda has certain key qualities that are to be found in many other places in Highland Scotland, highlighted in the examples listed above, **but nowhere are all of the qualities exhibited in the one place, except on the St Kilda archipelago**. Because of its extreme exposure to the North Atlantic, its isolation and remoteness, and the development of its unique cultural traditions, St Kilda cannot be likened to any other Scottish site:

- **The level of physical survival of features in the landscape of the archipelago is exceptional and our level of understanding of the society and their way of life through documentary sources is unsurpassed.**

- **The village on Hirta is without doubt the most complete and least altered site of its type in Highland Scotland.**

- **Nowhere else can be found that comes close to the ingenuity and sustainability of the St Kildans in their long-term relationship with the land and the seabirds.**

The impression that people from elsewhere had of the 'primitive' St Kildans provoked two almost opposing viewpoints. For those from nearby islands, the St Kildans were often seen as dirty and unsophisticated, and treated with contempt. Visitors from further afield, however, found it fascinating that these 'noble savages' were on Britain's doorstep. Both of these attitudes demonstrate that the people of St Kilda were perceived as being significantly different from their contemporaries both near and far.

1. Corbelled structures on Skellig Michael: corbelling technology was developed in prehistoric times in areas of Scotland and Ireland where timber was not available

2. *Cleit* corbelling

3. St Kilda Parliament (1927): Like the Dáil of the Blaskets, communal decision-making was a crucial part of the islanders' way of life

St Kilda •

• Tory Island

• Innishmurray

• Great Blasket/Skellig Michael

2

3

Irish seaboard islands

5

Although none are as remotely sited as St Kilda, the islands on the Atlantic seaboard off the west coast of Ireland are nevertheless well off the beaten track, and at various points in time housed thriving communities living in relative isolation. However, as the following reveals, all are quite different from the St Kilda archipelago and none have the unique range of qualities that survive so well on Hirta, Boreray, Soay, Dun and the nearby stacs.

5.1 Skellig Michael – World Heritage monastic retreat

The exceptional relict cultural landscape of Skellig Michael, abandoned as early as the 13th century AD, was inscribed on the World Heritage List in 1996.

The best surviving example of an isolated early medieval monastic island settlement on the Celtic fringe of Europe, Skellig Michael gives us clues about what a small part of Hirta might have looked like from around the 6th to 8th centuries AD. On Skellig Michael the monks occupied cellular

beehive structures made entirely from stone – in the absence of locally available wood. A spartan and very remote existence, they lived on birds, eggs and fish, along with produce from a sheltered monastic garden.

St Kilda also has various strands of evidence for the presence of an Early Christian monastic community, although as yet no structural remains of this period have been located. **But this is just one phase in 5000 years or more of St Kilda's history, and St Kilda displays many other special qualities not found on Skellig Michael.**

5.2 Great Blasket – centre of Irish Gaelic culture

Like St Kilda, Great Blasket has a long history of occupation, with a rich ethnographic record and a distinct social structure, and some similarities with St Kilda can usefully be explored. These similarities are, however, actually just very small parts in the overall nature of the place; when considered as a whole, St Kilda is far more significant. The following comparisons are included as examples:

- With a population of up to 176 in the past, Great Blasket was abandoned in 1953 after a steady decline. Just such a decline had taken place on St Kilda some 30 years earlier.

- Like St Kilda, the islanders on the Blaskets met every day at the 'Dáil' or Assembly, although this took place in the evening to discuss the day's events, rather than the St Kildan way which decided on the work plan at the start of the day.

- Although the arrangements of the villages differs, the 19th-century Blasket house-type looks similar to the 1861 'whitehouses' of Hirta's Village Bay – especially once felt became used for roofing, replacing reed thatch on the Blaskets and zinc sheeting on Hirta.

However, there are also very significant differences between Great Blasket and St Kilda:

- In the early 20th century, scholars visited and encouraged the Blasket islanders to document their folklore and traditions, and a strong Irish Gaelic culture was recorded for posterity – in music, poetry and prose. The oral and documentary record for St Kilda was gathered together on an *ad hoc* basis across many more centuries and is therefore very different in content and bias.

- Other than in times of food shortages, birds and their eggs were taken by the Blasket islanders more as a delicacy than as part of the staple diet. Seabirds were a fundamental part of the food-chain on St Kilda, and were an important means of 'paying' the rent.

- The 19th-century Blasket houses differed from those on the nearby mainland. In contrast, on Hirta it was the earlier structures that deviated from the mainland norm, with full integration of mainstream vernacular architectural styles from the 1830s onwards – with the exception of the *cleitean*, which continued to be built in their unique way.

The Blasket way of life does not compare to that on Hirta in terms of form and integrity, nor is there anything like the concentration or good preservation of monuments in the landscape as there is on Hirta as a whole.

5.3 Innishmurray – whiskey island

Innishmurray is a fairly typical example of the islands on the western seaboard of Ireland. It had a long history of occupation which ended in 1948 with the evacuation of the last 46 inhabitants. Although only four miles offshore, the island could nevertheless be cut off for long periods during winter, and on several days each summer.

Also like St Kilda, natural resources were relatively poor and restricted, but on Innishmurray the food supply was based on fish rather than birds. In the 19th century and up to the evacuation, however, the economy was mainly based on the sale of illicit whiskey – mirroring the St Kildan move away from subsistence produce from the late 19th century onwards, as a result of increasing contact or trade with the outside world.

> The cultural landscapes of Europe are among the world's richest, most diverse and complex heritage assets and their definition, classification and management are very difficult. WHC 1996

Whilst Innishmurray has some superficial similarities, St Kilda possesses a much greater number of features from all periods of human occupation; the preservation of the related structures on St Kilda is superb; and the associated documentary sources for the post-medieval period are much more extensive.

5.4 Tory Island – village fan

The distinctive arc of Village Bay on Hirta is a response to the form of the available landscape and the resources within it. A similar layout survives on Tory Island off the west coast of Ireland, where the arc of the village fits within a small area of land suitable for agriculture, and a fan of strip fields emanates from the house plots.

However, Hirta exhibits much more than just the parallel layout of village street, attached fields and seaside bay. It is an island with prehistoric and historic settlement patterns and closely associated agricultural divisions and evidence across its entirety, which itself is part of a wider archipelago providing vast food and rent resources, in the form of seabirds, extra grazing lands and places for seasonal or year-round occupation: a complete human ecological system.

5.5 Irish seaboard comparisons

The above examples represent relatively remote islands on the western seaboard of Ireland. Many were occupied for centuries or even millennia and then abandoned. A few exhibited some divergence in social organisation, music and the arts, and folklore, but for the most part little of this has been documented – with the notable exception of the Blaskets. **However, none of these places benefits from the St Kildan level of preservation of the evidence, both physically and in the writings of travellers. None compares favourably in terms of the time-depth of the landscape; the story of sustainability; the effects of extreme isolation in terms of divergence and local distinctiveness; nor St Kilda's later status reflecting a heroic community surviving in the face of adversity.**

1. *Cleitean* in the fields: a simple architectural response to the requirements of the place and the raw materials available

2. Skjaervaer, Vega: settlement in the vernacular tradition of the area; no buildings are more than 100-200 years old

3. The Factor's House, Hirta: those buildings with an official function were built by the distant landlord to mainland designs; until 1834, all other vernacular structures were built in the relatively primitive local style

> Cultural landscapes... represent a rich almost infinitely varied part of the human heritage... often reflect living models of sustainable use of land and natural resources.' Phillips 1995

North-west frontiers of Europe

6 Norse traders, travellers and warriors proved that the seemingly remote islands and fjords in the far north-west seaboard of Europe could sustain small populations, and supply sometimes exotic produce that was valued in the growing towns and cities of Europe and beyond. The last millennium in particular saw the establishment of isolated communities who found a living from the sea and the land. The harshness of the environment and the lack of opportunities often led to the abandonment of these outposts, although in some cases their products continued to have enough value to make it worthwhile to carry on the traditional land-uses of their ancestors: 'continuing cultural landscapes'.

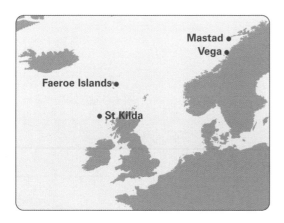

6.1 Vega – World Heritage cultural landscape

The Norwegian archipelago of Vega, inscribed to the World Heritage List in 2004, might appear to be one of the best places with which to compare and contrast St Kilda, but it is physically very much larger, with, historically, a far higher population that still exists today. Immediately there is, therefore, a difference in scale as well as in specific characteristics. In this, and many other ways, St Kilda is easily distinguished from the Vega World Heritage Site.

Vega eider houses and St Kildan *cleitean*: both are responses
to the special needs of the unusual subsistence economy

Like St Kilda, Vega has a long tradition of human settlement based on exploiting the fruits of the coastal environment. The unique economy, based strongly on eider ducks, led to the creation of the *e-hus* or *e-bane* – special eider duck houses. However, there was strong outside trading influence from early times, the eider down trade being controlled from at least the Norse period until the early 20th century. Thus Vega has strong cultural links with its trading partners in the ports of the Norwegian coast, contrasting with the isolation suffered on St Kilda. Vega also has a wide base of natural resources at its disposal, including access to large agricultural areas, and to rich fishing opportunities. This contrasts strongly with the St Kildan subsistence way of life which ended at the time of the evacuation in 1930.

Survival of vernacular settlements: The trading centre of Roroy on Vega reputedly remains much the same as when first established in the 18th century, and the interior and external architectural features reflect the power, wealth and distant cultural influence that came with trade. The Street on Hirta also reflects external influences of the time, and remains remarkably intact, but

represents an everyday vernacular building tradition at the opposite end of the spectrum from the higher status of Roroy. This difference is accentuated when other architectural forms are added to the equation – such as the bothies on Boreray and the shelters on Stac Li and Stac an Armin.

Eider down and eggs: The Vega archipelago was a key area for the development and operation of egg and down collecting, and up to a third of the annual income was based on this. Traces can still be found of many eider houses in which the birds would nest. These specialised structures are reminiscent of the drystone *cleitean* of St Kilda – some of which were also connected with fowling. The *cleitean,* however, are a unique feature of St Kilda: those found in steep boulder fields, on the stacs and at cliff edges, being where birds or bird eggs were stored and dried after catching.

The continuing cultural landscape of Vega is interesting to compare and contrast with St Kilda: it has a very long-established and thriving bird-based economy; the evidence of external influence survives well in places;

Puffin dogs of Mastad and Soay sheep of St Kilda:
isolated places allow genetic deviation, and also the
preservation of gene pools of enormous scientific value

its eider houses are a particular response to the natural resources; and there is a long history of human settlement. But Vega, sheltered from the ocean by an outer rim of islets and skerries, always owed its viability to fishing and trade, while the St Kildans were effectively on their own for most of the year, and relied almost entirely, for most of their history, on the scant resources they found around them. Both Vega and St Kilda could be classed as 'Globally Important Ingenious Agricultural Heritage Systems' as defined by United Nations Food Agricultural Organization (GIAHS; FAO 2002). Both systems, and their historical roots, should be, and are, cherished for what they tell us about, and what we can learn from, people's ingenuity to work with nature in a sustainable way. **However, St Kilda is easily distinguished from the Vega World Heritage Site by its subsistence way of life which ended in 1930, and the wealth and density of its very functional vernacular architecture, particularly the *cleitean* – a unique feature of the St Kilda archipelago.**

6.2 Mastad – isolated bird-based economy

'Their greatest treasure on earth...'

The village of Mastad and its immediate environs within Vaeroy of the Lofoten Islands, Norway, shares useful parallels with St Kilda, even though it is but a small part of the whole island. For the inhabitants of this remote community the seabirds that nested on the cliffs surrounding their village were their greatest treasure. They harvested the eggs and adult birds and salted the meat to last them through the winter. Puffin was the favourite meat, which they hunted with their unique six-toed puffin dog, but razorbills and guillemots were also caught in nets. As on St Kilda, the feathers provided a source of income from which they could buy imported goods. And like St Kilda, arable land was at a premium and the landscape forced a radial pattern of field systems with echoes of the village on Hirta. The lack of a proper harbour, and better opportunities elsewhere, resulted in the population declining from about 150 people until it was finally abandoned by its last inhabitant in 1974.

'Hidey hole' on Hirta: retreat was the best form of defence from lawless pirates and other unwelcome visitors

Sadly, the timber building tradition of Mastad means that few structures of significant age have survived, and their predecessors have left few traces of their former existence, whereas the stone building tradition of St Kilda has left the islands littered with evidence of use by countless generations of islanders.

The restricted area of this isolated bird-based economy and the lack of upstanding evidence for time-depth contrasts with that for **St Kilda – a seabird economy par excellence within an agricultural landscape which, taken as a whole, is of extraordinary cultural value.**

6.3 Faeroe Islands – remote trading posts

Although not comparable to St Kilda in terms of their size and much greater number of islands, the Faeroe Islands are relatively remote, and largely dependent on the rich resources of the North Atlantic, sometimes relying heavily on fowling. Their timber drying sheds, the *hjallur,* are similar in purpose to the St Kildan *cleitean:* for drying and preserving mutton, fish and seabirds to last them through the winter. However, the Faeroes are much richer in resources, and much less isolated in terms of trade and communications, and therefore more in tune with regional society, culture and traditions.

Hidey holes: The folklore of the Faeroes tells of small shelters – *fransatoftir* – where people hid from pirates. Such structures are still to be found in the rocky screes of St Kilda: these 'hidey holes' are virtually invisible and are recorded as having been used to hide from unwelcome visitors to the village.

Local tradition: As in most landscapes, the place-names of the Faeroes are sometimes associated with myths and legends. A pregnant milkmaid called Malan, for instance, when teased for not keeping up with the others, is said to have picked up a 176kg rock and challenged others to do the same. Calum Mor's house on St Kilda has a similar story of strength: it is said to have been built in a day by Calum to prove his manliness.

Calum Mor's House, Hirta: a complete survivor from before the 19th century, associated with the legend of Calum Mor

6.4 North-west European comparisons

Even these seemingly very remote places on the north-west outskirts of Europe were in fact once part of a thriving and well-established trading network, and almost everywhere relied on trade rather than the basic subsistence practised on St Kilda. This is explained by St Kilda's location – well off the beaten track, and with too few commodities to be worth the detour. The bounty of the seas was also used elsewhere to support the mixed land-based agriculture, whereas St Kildans treated the treacherous surrounding seas with caution and respect, and took very little in the way of fish, seals or whales. But perhaps the most significant resource difference was the availability of timber – to build houses, boats, fences, and to make everyday items. With no home-grown timber, and little coming in through trade or even as driftwood, elements of the unusual architectural tradition of St Kilda continued until the archipelago was evacuated in 1930.

Ahu Tongariki, Rapa Nui

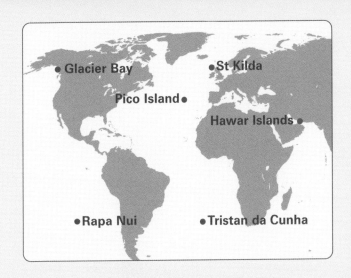

> Man used to have a harmonious and respectful relation with Nature. He used to be humble and knew that he was dependent on Nature. Feliu 2003

The global experience

7

Part of the iconic status of St Kilda relates to its profound feeling of remoteness and isolation. In European terms it is certainly unusually far from the nearest major landfall, to the extent that the medieval writer John of Fordun (c.1380) thought it was '... on the margine of the world ...'. King James IV (1473-1513) thought St Kilda was even too remote to include within his kingdom!

The story of sustainability is one that can be compared and contrasted with other remote places in the world, where responses to limited natural resources could also be ingenious – though very different to St Kilda. Equally interesting are the stories of unsustainable practices and the influence of outsiders leading to the demise of previously sustainable ways of life.

However, such comparisons do not bear close scrutiny: it is only helpful to look at individual characteristics or similarities: nowhere could be found to parallel the range of outstanding features that makes St Kilda so extraordinary.

Rapa Nui – diminishing resources and isolated society

The World Heritage Site of Rapa Nui – the most remote inhabited place in the world – is famous for the unsustainable consequences of its religious practices; practices that are recorded in the monumental sculptures and sacred sites that still survive on the island. **Conversely, St Kilda is famous for its *sustainable* practices, which only became too difficult through external influences, and when the population fell below a certain level**. The natural resources on which the St Kildan's survived continue to be available today.

St Kilda
a comparative analysis of the cultural landscape
Summary

1. Tristan da Cunha from the air: topographically resembling St Kilda, but culturally worlds apart

2-3. Currais on Pico and the An Lag exclosures on Hirta: devising special responses to the geology, topography and climate was essential to the sustainability of both agricultural systems

4-5. Tlingit and St Kildan women selling their local wares and souvenirs (1880s and 1894): tourism may have seemed like a life-line, but was also a noose which tightened round the old ways of life

6. Hawar: good for settlement and harvesting rich natural food resources

Tristan da Cunha – remote outliers

St Kilda and the remote South Atlantic island group of Tristan da Cunha both relied heavily on the seabird harvest, and used adjacent islands for some of their grazing animals. Both island groups suffered from a lack of communications, and have similar histories of emigration and boating disasters. But Tristan da Cunha lacks the cultural time-depth of St Kilda – with just 200 years of human settlement, and the preservation of the cultural landscape of St Kilda is in no way matched by its South Atlantic counterpart. **St Kilda has a time-depth that reflects 5000 years of human occupation, with a density of structural and agricultural evidence which is quite astounding.**

Pico Island, Azores – specialist building traditions

The remote island community of Pico developed a local way of life to suit the seemingly barren hills of their home. Parts of the island are covered in *currais* – distinctive stone-walled enclosures for sheltering the growing vines, reminiscent, in terms of density and divergent architectural style, to the *cleitean* of St Kilda. However, the Azores were only settled from the mid-15th century,

and their economy is based on trade rather than the self-sufficient way of life of St Kilda. As well as the vineyards, the Pico islanders had rich farming, whaling, fishing, and woodland – all of which contributed to economic sustainability.

The World Heritage Site of Pico Island exhibits just 500 years of settlement history which was sustained by a vigorous trading system. **St Kilda has a considerably greater time-depth and an isolated self-sufficiency that meant that its lack of economic partners was unimportant**.

Glacier Bay, Alaska – external social influences

The story of the abandonment of the native Tlingit villages in the 19th century has parallels with St Kilda. The Tlingit experience of huge external influence is mirrored on St Kilda by the remodelling of the village, by the effects of diseases brought in by outsiders, and by the ability of the St Kildans to adapt to new ways of life. The evidence of this on St Kilda is contained within the rich documentary record, and in the physical remains that are spread across the whole landscape.

> A cultural landscape is a memorial to the unknown labourer. Fowler 2001

The Glacier Bay story is characterised by the strength of socio-economic changes enforced on the population in the 19th century by landlord/magnates. **St Kilda also went through major socio-economic changes but they were not all-embracing, nor were they introduced purely for the profit of the landlord.**

Hawar Islands, Bahrain – an abandoned bird economy

Little documentation remains of the subsistence economy that once characterised Hawar, where the inhabitants exploited birds and their eggs as well as shellfish and fish stocks. It was not until the late 1960s that the physical isolation and the lack of healthcare and educational facilities made the fishing villages of southern and western Bahrain more tempting, and the islands were largely deserted.

Until comparatively recently the Hawar Islands supported a vibrant society dependent on its seabirds, but the influence of modern society led to the abandonment of the traditional ways. **St Kilda was similarly dependent on its seabirds, but** **although it too has been abandoned, the upstanding evidence for the past way of life remains incredibly rich and dense.**

The global context

Although World Heritage cultural landscapes tend mainly to reflect the distinctive characteristics of their own geo-cultural region, it has been illuminating to look at St Kilda in the context of a few other remote communities around the world. In this comparison we can see that, although based on different agricultural systems and from a different cultural background, St Kilda is an extremely well-preserved example of a phenomenon that continues to the present day: communities living 'on the edge' in subsistence economies which only fail, or are threatened by failure, because of external influences, rather than because the inhabitants have acted unsustainably: Rapa Nui being the exception that proves the rule. It is essential that we recognise and cherish the best-preserved examples of such cultural landscapes in different regions of the world, as reminders of the importance of maintaining our balance with nature.

1. Boreray and the Stacs – the
   source of many of the thousands
   of seabirds the St Kildans relied
   on for food, light and rent

2. Possibly prehistoric boat-shaped
   setting, with the island of Boreray
   in the background

3. Islanders loading their
   possessions on the day of
   evacuation of the islands: 29th
   August 1930

4. Drystone enclosures and cleits
   adjoining the 'head dyke'

1

Cultural landscape links past with future

Fowler 2004

Conclusions

8

This additional comparative analysis has been a helpful exercise, which has set St Kilda more firmly in its regional and wider context. The analysis has established the links with other islands in the same geo-cultural location and set out some similarities. However, the analysis has also highlighted clear and distinct differences between St Kilda and other north European islands and other remote communities.

The places that have been considered here are all important cultural landscapes, and some include acknowledged features of 'outstanding universal value', but **no place in the world has been found which better demonstrates the unique combination of features that makes St Kilda recognised around the world as an icon of remote island living and sustainable subsistence. St Kilda is therefore ideally placed to represent remote island culture in the north-west Atlantic coast of Europe.**

What has emerged is that St Kilda is linked culturally to several other sites: the difference is that St Kilda exhibits a greater range of qualities, and exhibits those qualities better than other places. St Kilda can be seen as representative of a type of isolated island culture, but is the best exemplar of this in having qualities in such abundance as well as the evocative spiritual qualities associated with its remoteness, isolation and aesthetic landscape qualities.

Happy St Kildan children in 1909: those who survived were evacuated from the islands on 29 August 1930

While many of the places cited above have fascinating stories to tell, their stories belong to a significantly different cultural tradition. St Kilda retains the most complete physical legacy of this type of tiny island community, dwarfed by nature yet able to live in harmony with its environment until the values and influences of the wider world made the islanders' way of life untenable. The iconic St Kilda story of sustainability followed by abandonment catches the imagination of people from around the world. Today, visitors can still stand in the village street and easily imagine the community in its heyday, an experience that touches the heart of everyone who has made the pilgrimage to the island 'at the edge of the world'.

Several existing World Heritage Sites were considered in this comparative analysis, but none were found to cover the same qualities as St Kilda. Some are 'globally important ingenious agricultural heritage systems', but all have significantly different characteristics from St Kilda. The conclusion is that the tangible and intangible inheritance, preserved so well on this small group of tiny, remote islands, is not currently represented on the World Heritage List.

Bibliography

FAO, 2002, 'Globally Important, Ingenious Agricultural Heritage Systems (GIAHS). First Stakeholder Workshop and Steering Committee Session, Rome, 5-7 August 2002', United Nations Food and Agriculture Organisation, Paris

von Droste, B., Plachter, H. and Rössler, M., (eds), 1995, *Cultural Landscapes of Universal Value: Components of a Global Stategy,* G. Fischer, Stuttgart

Feliu, C.A., 2003, 'Cultural Landscapes: Evaluating the Interaction Between People and Nature' in WHC 2003, 37-9

Fleming, A., 2000, 'St Kilda: Family, Community, and the Wider World', *J. Anthropol. Archaeol.* 19, 348-68

Fowler, P.J., 2001, 'Cultural landscapes: great concept, pity about the phrase', in *The Cultural Landscape. Planning for a sustainable partnership between people and place,* London: ICOMOS-UK, 64-82

Fowler, P.J., 2003, *World Heritage Cultural Landscapes 1992-2002,* World Heritage Papers 6, UNESCO World Heritage Centre, Paris

Fowler, P.J., 2004, *Landscapes of the World: Conserving a Global Heritage,* Windgather Press, Macclesfield

MacCulloch, J., 1819, *A Description of the Western Isles of Scotland 2,* Robinson and Co., London

Martin, M., 1698, A Late Voyage to St Kilda, London

Phillips, A., 1995, 'Cultural Landscapes: an IUCN Perspective', in von Droste *et al.,* 380-392

WHC 1996, 'Report on the Expert Meeting on European Cultural Landscapes of Outstanding Universal Value (Vienna, Austria, 21 April 1996)' WHC-96/CONF.208/INF.12, UNESCO World Heritage Centre, Paris

WHC 2003, Cultural Landscapes: the *Challenges of Conservation,* World Heritage Papers 7, UNESCO World Heritage Centre, Paris

Acknowledgements

This document was written and compiled by Robin Turner, Jill Harden and Susan Bain of the National Trust for Scotland who would like to thank the following people for their help and assistance:
Steve Boyle, Peter Burman, Susan Denyer, Caitlin Evans, Sally Foster, Peter Fowler, Annemarie Gibson, Alex Hale, Colin MacConnachie, Ian MacKenzie, Lyn Turner, Finlay West, Steven Wiseman, Susan Williamson, Manson Wright, Christopher Young and to staff at Astron, particularly John Maxwell and the Graphic Design Team

Image Acknowledgements

The following sources of images in this document are gratefully acknowledged:
Susan Bain
Colin Baxter
Niall Benvie
Mike Brooks
Andrew Fleming
Jill Harden
Mary Harman
John Love
Richard Luxmoore
Alistair Mackay
Dag Sorli
Robin Turner
Stephen Wiseman
Kris and Ana @lifeisgrand
Aerofilms
Collection of the Society of Writers to Her Majesty's Signet, National Archives of Scotland
Directorate for Nature Management, Norway
GUARD
Maclean Press
National Trust for Scotland
RCAHMS
University of Aberdeen
University of Washington Library